MIDLOTHIAN PUBLIC LIBRARY

3 1614 00187

P9-CCG-896

MYSTERY HUNTERS

FAKES AND HOAXES

Sarah Levete

MIDLOTHIAN PUBLIC LIBRARY
14701 S. KENTON AVENUE
MIDLOTHIAN, IL 60445

Gareth Stevens
PUBLISHING

Please visit our website, www.garethstevens.com.
For a free color catalog of all our high-quality books,
call toll free 1-800-542-2595 of fax 1-877-542-2596.

Cataloging-in-Publication Data
Names: Levete, Sarah.
Title: Fakes and hoaxes / Sarah Levete.
Description: New York : Gareth Stevens, 2017. | Series: Mystery hunters | Includes index.
Identifiers: ISBN 9781482460049 (pbk.) | ISBN 9781482460063 (library bound) |
    ISBN 9781482460056 (6 pack)
Subjects: LCSH: Hoaxes--Case studies--Juvenile literature. | Impostors and imposture--Juvenile
    literature. | Deception--Juvenile literature.
Classification: LCC CT9980.L48 2017 | DDC 001.9'5--dc23

First Edition

Published in 2017 by
Gareth Stevens Publishing
111 East 14th Street, Suite 349
New York, NY 10003

Copyright © 2017 Gareth Stevens Publishing

Produced for Gareth Stevens by Calcium
Editors: Sarah Eason and Claudia Martin
Picture researcher: Rachel Blount
Designer: Emma DeBanks

Picture credits: Cover: Shutterstock: Katja Gerasimova tr, Victor Habbick c, Diana Hlevnjak bl;
Inside: Flickr: Rich Griffith 26–27b, Taylor Herring 19b; Shutterstock: Adike 25b, AlenKadr 36–
37bg, Esteban De Armas 14–15bg, Marilyn Barbone 32b, Belizar 6b, M. BestGreenScreen 16–17,
Linda Bucklin 18b, Butterflybrain 20b, Catmando 18–19bg, Chromakey 36b, Cornelius 4–5bg,
Cranach 8–9bg, Everett Historical 8–9c, 34b, Featureflash Photo Agency 38t, Fona 20–21bg,
22–23bg, Fer Gregory 5t, 6–7, Victor Habbick 12b, Diana Hlevnjak 10–11bg, Elsa Hoffmann
42br, HomeArt 40–41bg, ID1974 30–31bg, IM_photo 38–39b, Kostyantyn Ivanyshen 10–11,
Jezper 34–35bg, Evgeny Karandaev 42–43bg, Barandash Karandashich 21t, Thomas Koch 42bl,
Michelle Lalancette 8–9t, Lazyllama 24–25bg, Lendy16 41b, Lightspring 26–27bg, Megaflopp
41t, Mellimage 40r, Natural Earth Imagery 1, 42–43t, Neftali 32–33bg, Nicolas Primola 11t,
Jeremy Reddington 33r, Michael Rosskothen 14l, Arjen de Ruiter 28–29bg, Samzsolti 4, Alinute
Silzeviciute 12–13bg, Sruilk 15t, Tonhom1009 17t, Popova Valeriya 30b, Monika Wisniewska 38–
39bg; Wikimedia Commons:, Eviatar Bach 22–23t, Didier Descouens 28–29t, (The book's text by
JF Nicholls (d. 1883) and John Taylor (d. 1893); unknown engravers) 31r, Mike Peel 28b, Romanov
family 35t, Henry Louis Stephens (1824-82) 23b, Nancy Wong 37t.

All rights reserved. No part of this book may be reproduced in any form without permission from
the publisher, except by reviewer.

Printed in China

CPSIA compliance information: Batch #CW17GS: For further information contact Gareth Stevens, New York, New York at 1-800-542-2595.

CONTENTS

Chapter 1

CAN YOU BELIEVE IT?

Do you believe everything you read, see, or hear? Do you ever wonder if someone is playing a trick on you? For hundreds of years, people have carried out harmless and often humorous **hoaxes**. From lies about seeing monsters to carefully planned tricks that fool thousands of people, this book looks at some of the world's most fascinating fakes and hoaxes.

Fact or Fiction?

Where hoaxes and fakes are concerned, it takes detective work to find the truth. Sometimes, there is no clear answer as to whether something is a hoax or real. Some elaborate hoaxes and fakes are based on information that is presented as fact. At first glance, the fact seems to be convincing. Only after further investigation do people realize they have been fooled!

No one is sure what an alien looks like. Could this one be the real thing?

Do monsters live beneath the waters of lakes and seas? Or are they just hoaxes?

Monsters, Myths, and Magic

There are many hoaxes about monsters, **myths**, and even magic. Some of the stories are ancient and others more modern. The hoax creators have tricked some people into believing the stories are true, and created debate among others. Despite scientific **evidence** to disprove many hoaxes, there are some people who choose to believe they are true. Find out more about fakes and hoaxes that have captured the imagination of people around the world. Remember as you read: a hoax or fake should never be carried out with the intention of making fun of someone, harming anyone, or making money.

MYSTERY HUNTER

Look for the Mystery Hunter boxes throughout the book. They will ask you to look at the information given in each chapter and answer questions based on what you have read. Then turn to pages 44–45 to see if your answer is correct.

Fooled!

In many parts of the world, there is a special day on which people are encouraged to play harmless **pranks**, humorously tricking others into believing something that is not true. This is April 1, known as April Fools' Day, or All Fools' Day. When the victim falls for the prank, the prankster shouts "April Fool!"

Perfect Pet!

In 1984, the *Orlando Sentinel* newspaper reported on a small creature, about 4 inches (10 cm) long, called the Tasmanian mock walrus. The article said the animal looked like a walrus and sounded like a purring cat! It was a perfect pet because it never needed cleaning, ate pesky cockroaches, and used a litter box. However, pest-control businesses wanted these pets banned because they were worried that no one would pay for their services to get rid of cockroaches anymore. People contacted the *Orlando Sentinel* wanting to find out where to purchase a mock walrus. It is unlikely any of them would have been able to do so, because the article appeared on April 1!

A photograph of a naked mole rat illustrated the hoax article about the "perfect pet."

Does Money Really Grow on Trees?

In 1963, an American magazine called *View* tricked its readers into believing that dollars grow on trees. According to the magazine, a yenom tree belonging to Mrs. Loo Flirpa began to sprout not just flowers, but freshly grown dollar bills. Mrs. Loo Flirpa took advantage of her extraordinary luck by agreeing a deal with the U.S. Mint and Federal Reserve, which are responsible for making dollar bills, to sell seedlings from her money-making tree. The amazing story was actually a hoax created for April Fools' Day. (Try spelling Loo Flirpa backward!)

Would you believe that money grows on trees?

MYSTERIOUS FACTS

April Fools' Day is celebrated in many countries, from France, where it is called *poissons d'avril* (April fish), to India:

- In the United States, April Fools' Day pranks last all day, but in other countries they take place only until noon.

- The origin of April Fools' Day is not clear but it has been linked to ancient festivals such as a Roman festival called "hilaria."

- Some people believe the **tradition** started when the French changed the start of the year from April to January in 1564. People played jokes on those who refused to stop celebrating New Year at the start of April.

True, False, or Unknown?

Before the invention of the TV or the Internet, people listened to the radio for entertainment. One Sunday evening in the United States, on October 30, 1938, millions of people tuned into the radio station Colombia Broadcasting Corporation (CBC). They were in for a shock.

Aliens on Earth!

Listeners were horrified when a radio news announcer stated that aliens from outer space had landed on Earth. Some people panicked and rushed out of their homes. In fact, aliens had not landed: CBC was actually broadcasting an adaptation of the book *The War of the Worlds* by the science-fiction writer H. G. Wells (1866–1946)!

The program was not meant to trick people, but some listeners had tuned in halfway through, so they had not heard the program announcer explain that the broadcast was a drama. Some listeners believed a real alien attack was taking place, although the extent of the panic may have been exaggerated by newspaper reporters!

Wolf Alert

During the 2014 Winter Olympics in Sochi, Russia, there were many reports of stray dogs wandering the streets. So, when U.S. **luger** Kate Hansen posted a video to **social media** showing a wolf in the Olympic Village sleeping areas, it was taken seriously and reported by newspapers. However, the video was a hoax planned and carried out by comedian Jimmy Kimmel, working with Kate Hansen. Kimmel and his TV crew had built a copy of an Olympic Village corridor and dorm in a TV studio, where they videoed a wolf that they had rented! Twenty-four hours after posting the video, the pair revealed the truth.

Some people believed that a wolf really was prowling through Sochi in 2014!

The Angel of Mons

During World War I (1914–1918), at the Battle of Mons in Belgium, British soldiers were under fierce attack from the Germans. According to later newspaper reports, many exhausted British soldiers saw visions of angels in the sky. According to these reports, the sight of the angels kept the Germans from advancing farther. The battle took place in August 1914. Yet no one heard about the angels until after September 29, 1914, when a writer named Arthur Machen had a short story called "The Bowmen" published in the *London Evening News*. The story, which Machen never meant to be seen as anything but fiction, was about visions at the Battle of Mons. Was the **legend** of the "Angel of Mons" all started by a short story, or did some soldiers really see visions?

The World War I battlefields were bleak and terrifying places.

MYSTERY HUNTER

Based on the information you have read about the Angel of Mons, what historical evidence could you use to explain why the British public might want to believe in the visions? Give reasons for your answer.

Chapter 2

MONSTROUS WORLD

Do you believe the tales of long-necked monsters lurking in the inky depths of the ocean or huge beasts roaming through thick, dark forests? For decades, people have wondered whether faded, grainy photographs of giant beasts and reported sightings of unknown creatures are real or fake. Until these monsters are exposed as hoaxes or identified as a **species** of animal, people will continue to wonder whether or not they are real. How can scientists ever prove that a monster does or does not exist?

Is this creature a monster, or simply an as-yet-unidentified species?

The Study of Monsters

The study of unknown "creatures" is called cryptozoology. This is the search for creatures that most people believe are myths or even fakes. These creatures are known as **cryptids**. Some of the animals we are familiar with today, such as the striped okapi (a cross between a horse and zebra), were once thought to be imaginary. For centuries, locals in the South Asian islands of Indonesia talked of a huge dragon-like creature. In 1912, an expedition of scientists from the United States discovered several of these large-headed creatures and identified them as a new species of animal. It was the world's largest living lizard, which scientists named the Komodo dragon.

The duck-billed platypus is a strange-looking creature that scientists once believed was a hoax!

It's Real!

During the nineteenth century, scientists were sometimes fooled by hoaxes. The people responsible for the hoaxes tricked scientists into thinking there was a new species of animal by sewing the body parts of different animals together! For that reason, when scientists at the British Museum, London, England, were sent a creature that had a furry body, a duck's bill, the feet of an otter, and a tail like a beaver, they thought it was a joke. However, it wasn't! This weird-looking creature was the Australian animal now known as the duck-billed platypus.

MYSTERIOUS FACTS

New species of animals are still being discovered. "Monsters" or mythical beasts may just be unidentified animals:

- The Chacoan peccary was known from **fossils** but it was thought to be extinct, until it was discovered living in Argentina in 1971.

- Until 1902, the mountain gorilla was thought to be imaginary. It was only discovered to be real when German army officer Friedrich Robert von Beringe shot two of the animals! The species was named *Gorilla beringei* for its discoverer.

Nessie

Loch Ness is a lake in Scotland, in the United Kingdom, measuring 22 miles (36 km) long and 1.5 miles (2.4 km) wide. Its waters are inky black. Beneath the surface, it is hard to see farther than 4 inches (10 cm). Many people believe the loch is home to the Loch Ness Monster, commonly known as "Nessie." Others think the monster is a myth that has been helped along by hoax sightings and photographs.

Mysterious Monk

According to legend, rumors of a monster lurking in the lake began in the sixth century. A monk is reported to have saved the life of a man who was attacked by a strange creature in the loch. The belief continued but was never proven. In 1933, a road was built around the lake. This sparked yet more sightings from people saying they had seen a huge dinosaur-like creature in the water.

*Plesiosaurs lived 220 million years ago. Could Nessie be a **descendant**?*

In 1933, Hugh Gray took the first photograph of what looked like a monster in the loch. However, many people said it was Gray's dog swimming in the water! In 1943, Dr. Robert Kenneth Wilson took a photograph of the Loch Ness Monster that was published in a British newspaper, the *Daily Mail*. However, 30 years later, the *Sunday Telegraph* newspaper revealed that the photograph was a fake, created using a toy submarine!

Further Research

There have been plenty of well-known hoaxes about Nessie, but the belief in the monster's existence still remains. Scientists have tried countless ways to find the monster, using everything from submarines to **sonar**.

Some people think that images of Nessie look similar to the plesiosaur, a type of sea reptile that lived 220 million years ago. They think that Nessie is a species of large animal that is still to be identified. Such a case has happened before. For example, the coelacanth is a fish that was once thought to have been extinct for millions of years. It was only when a live specimen was caught off the coast of South Africa in 1938 that scientists learned that the fish still existed.

Every year, over a million people visit Loch Ness.

Monster Tales

Ancient tales of a sea monster named the Kraken have frightened sailors for centuries. It was said that this creature of the deep could toss a ship into the wild waves, hurling sailors to their death. Could this deadly sea monster—reported to be over 30 feet (9 m) long and able to eat a whale in one gulp—be real? Or might its terrifying reputation actually be a case of mistaken identity or overactive imaginations?

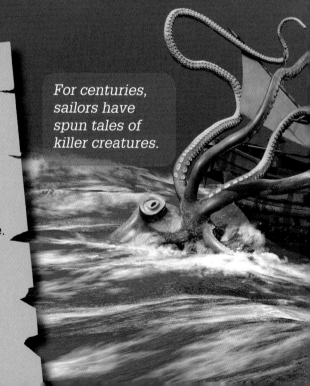

Deep-Sea Evidence

In 1857, the Danish **naturalist** Japetus Steenstrup (1813–1897) looked into the tales of the mysterious deep-sea monster. He examined the beak of a large squid, about 3 inches (8 cm) across, which had washed up on Denmark's shores. Steenstrup figured out that the beak must come from an enormous squid up to 46 feet (14 m) long. He started to believe that this might be the mysterious Kraken that fishermen warned of ...

MYSTERIOUS FACTS

Could sightings of the "Kraken" actually be glimpses of deep-sea squid?

- Giant squid have eight arms, covered with suction cups. These are lined with horny rings with sharp teeth. Once a victim is in a squid's grip, it cannot escape.

- The colossal squid is the largest species of squid. As Steenstrup estimated, it can grow 46 feet (14 m) long. It lives in the deep ocean, where it preys on huge sperm whales.

For centuries, sailors have spun tales of killer creatures.

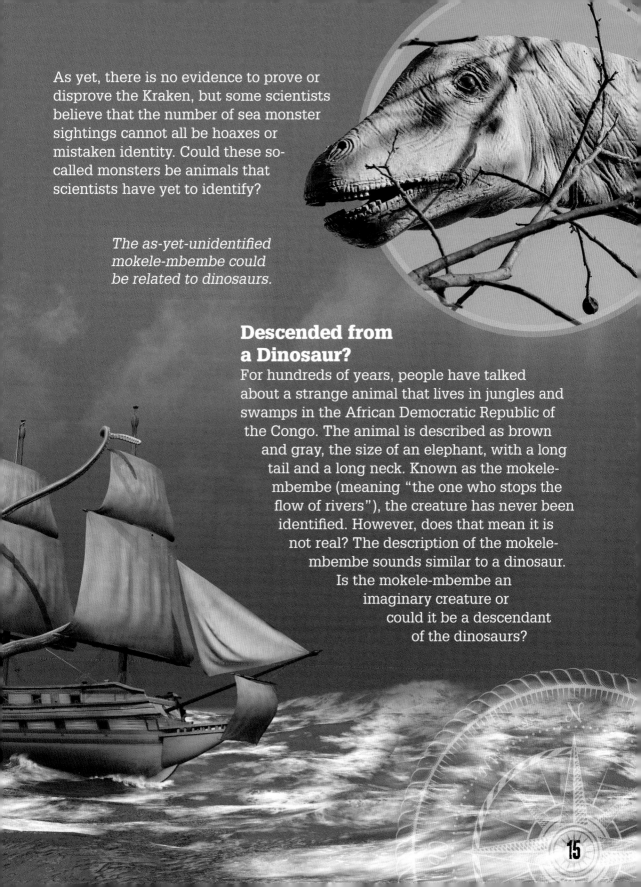

As yet, there is no evidence to prove or disprove the Kraken, but some scientists believe that the number of sea monster sightings cannot all be hoaxes or mistaken identity. Could these so-called monsters be animals that scientists have yet to identify?

The as-yet-unidentified mokele-mbembe could be related to dinosaurs.

Descended from a Dinosaur?

For hundreds of years, people have talked about a strange animal that lives in jungles and swamps in the African Democratic Republic of the Congo. The animal is described as brown and gray, the size of an elephant, with a long tail and a long neck. Known as the mokele-mbembe (meaning "the one who stops the flow of rivers"), the creature has never been identified. However, does that mean it is not real? The description of the mokele-mbembe sounds similar to a dinosaur. Is the mokele-mbembe an imaginary creature or could it be a descendant of the dinosaurs?

What's in a Name?

It is a cross between an ape, a bear, and a human. It is huge and hairy, its feet are enormous, and it appears in remote areas of the world—but no one knows for sure what it is. There is a long-standing belief that such a creature lives in the snowy mountains of the Himalayas, where it is known as a Yeti. It is also thought to wander through forests in North America, where it is known as Bigfoot. Are these strange beasts legends, based on little more than imagination, or are they really monsters? Perhaps they are simply animals, such as bears, that are mistaken for monsters?

Strange Sightings

In 1951, the British mountaineer Eric Shipton came back from an expedition to Mount Everest. He brought with him photographs of giant footprints imprinted in the snow. The legend of the so-called Yeti began. Meanwhile, in North America, a legend about a giant beast named Bigfoot was underway, after some huge and unexplained footprints were spotted there, too.

Some areas where Bigfoot or the Yeti have reportedly been seen have become tourist destinations. The local people often encourage visitors to search for the monsters so that they will spend money on accommodation and food while they are there.

Tests, such as analyzing hair samples, help scientists hunt down the truth about monsters like Bigfoot or the Yeti.

Testing, Testing

Some of the sightings and "evidence" of Bigfoot or the Yeti are now believed to be hoaxes. Ray Wallace, one of the people who claimed he had seen Bigfoot, actually owned some large wooden feet! A blurred video taken on a cell phone by two 11-year-olds in snowy Siberia, Russia, shows the shape of a Yeti. However, many people say the video is a hoax. In an attempt to uncover the truth, a three-year research study by scientists at Oxford University, England, examined "evidence" such as strands of hair and pieces of feces, which had been sent from around the world. The scientists decided that none of the evidence proved the monster existed. However, Bryan Sykes, a researcher on the project, said: "The fact that none of these samples turned out to be [Bigfoot] doesn't mean the next one won't." Perhaps Bigfoot does exist after all!

MYSTERY HUNTER

Based on the evidence in this chapter, do you think that Bigfoot, the Yeti, and the Loch Ness Monster are monsters, hoaxes, or unidentified species of animal?

Chapter 3

MYTHICAL BEINGS

Most cultures have their own myths. A myth is a traditional story that is often used to explain natural happenings, such as thunder and lightning, or to explain why something exists, such as an elephant's long trunk. Myths are not based on historical or scientific evidence—they are simply stories passed down from one generation to another. However, some people have created elaborate hoaxes to make others believe that myths are, in fact, real.

Magical Unicorns

Many children's stories feature magical horse-like creatures called unicorns. These elegant white animals have a single horn and mysterious powers. The unicorn is generally agreed to be a fictional animal. However, during the 1500s, the horns from single-horned whales called narwhals were sometimes sold as unicorn horns. People paid a lot of money for them because of their so-called magical powers.

The narwhal tusk is an enlarged tooth!

In the 1600s, a German scientist named Otto von Guericke (1602–1686) found ancient animal bones in a cave. He decided they belonged to a unicorn, and drew a diagram of how the beast must have looked. For over a century, many people believed the bones to be a genuine unicorn skeleton, but they were later proved to belong to many different animals, including a rhinoceros, a mammoth, and a narwhal. Even today, some people still believe in unicorns. For example, in 1991, an Austrian naturalist named Antal Festetics claimed to have seen and filmed a unicorn. Other **footage** of creatures that look like unicorns exists, but none of these films has yet been proven to be genuine.

Beached Dragon

In 2013, people enjoying a day on the beach in Dorset, in the United Kingdom, were amazed to find a massive 40-foot (12-m) dragon's skull on the sand. One hundred years ago, some people might have thought the skull was real. Today, very few adults believe that dragons exist, so no one was fooled—but they were intrigued! It turned out that the skull was an incredible sculpture that had taken a **special effects** team two months to create. The team was not trying to trick anyone: the stunt was an advertisement for an adults' TV program called *Game of Thrones*. The popular **fantasy** show features dragons, magic, and monsters.

If you came across this giant skull on a beach, would you think it was a hoax?

Fairy Magic

Fairies sprinkle fairy dust and live in woods and under mushrooms! From the tooth fairy to elves, fairies are simply wonderful imaginary creatures—or are they? In the early twentieth century, evidence surfaced that seemed to prove that these delicate beings actually existed.

Photographic Evidence

In 1917, two young cousins named Elsie Wright (1901–1988) and Frances Griffiths (1907–1986) borrowed a camera from Elsie's father to take photographs at the bottom of their backyard, in Cottingley, in the United Kingdom. Elsie's father developed the photographs in his **dark room**. In the pictures, he saw the cousins with what seemed to be fairies. Knowing that his daughter was a good artist, he dismissed the pictures as a trick.

I Believe in Fairies!

However, when Elsie's mother, who was interested in the **supernatural**, came across the images, she believed them to show genuine, delicate-winged fairies. She showed the photographs to other people. They eventually came to the attention of Arthur Conan Doyle (1859–1930), the author of the famous Sherlock Holmes detective novels. Doyle also had a strong belief in the supernatural. He wrote a magazine article stating that the photographs were indeed the real thing! Some people accepted the fairy images as genuine, but many others still had doubts.

Many legends and tales feature fairies and spells.

It was not until the
1980s, when the cousins
were elderly ladies,
that they admitted
the photographs
were fakes. Elsie
and Frances had used
simple paper cut-out
images of fairies, which
they then photographed!

Fairy Child

As a child, Dora Kunz
(1904–1999) claimed
that she played with and
talked to fairies. Later, she
wrote a book called *The
Real World of Fairies* based
on her experiences. Kunz
recorded that in 1979 she saw
fairies in Central Park in New
York City. However, according to
Kunz, the increasing levels of pollution
in the city made it harder to interact with
these nature spirits.

MYSTERIOUS FACTS

According to myth, there are several
types of fairies:

- Elves live under the ground,
  partying, dancing, and playing music.
  They kidnap people who are caught
  listening to their music.

- Flower fairies dress like young
  girls and spread the scent of flowers
  as they dance.

- Goblins are naughty fairies. They
  have bulging eyes and strangely
  shaped bodies.

*Not all fairies
are good. Some
enjoy tricking
humans!*

21

This merman is on show in Banff, Canada. No one is sure where it came from.

Mysterious Mermaids

Mermaids and mermen are half-human, half-fish beings that are said to live in the deep ocean. For centuries, there have been reported sightings of merpeople. Perhaps some of these sightings are a case of mistaken identity. Some people think that ocean-dwelling **mammals** such as dolphins, porpoises, and manatees may have been mistaken for merpeople.

The Fiji Mermaid

In 1822, American sea captain Samuel Eades landed on an island where he saw the body of a mermaid, which was for sale. Eades decided to buy it, and sold his ship to pay for it. He took the mermaid to England. A naturalist confirmed that the body was genuinely a mermaid. Eades displayed the body and people paid to see it. However, another scientist soon declared the body and head to be that of an orangutan attached to the tail of a salmon. The mermaid was a hoax!

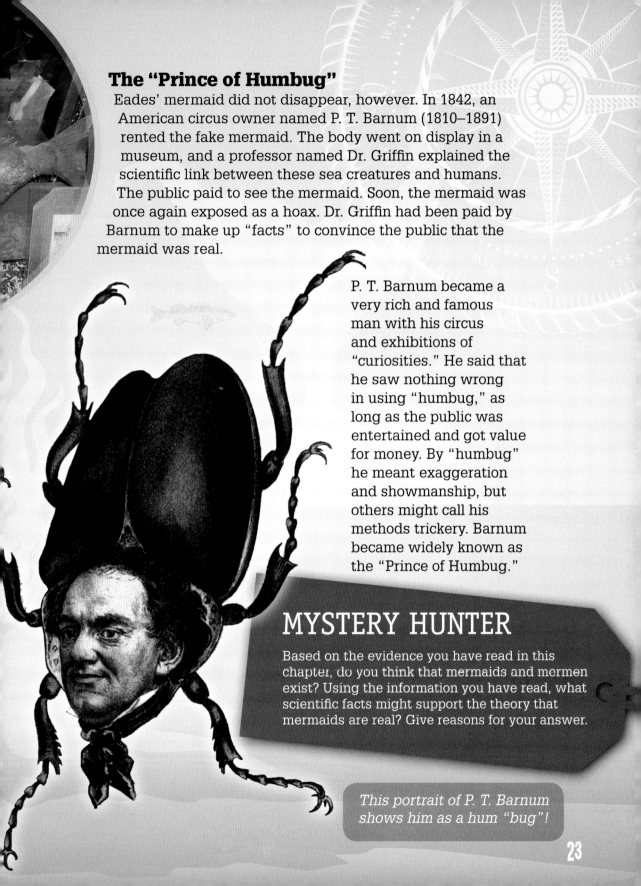

The "Prince of Humbug"

Eades' mermaid did not disappear, however. In 1842, an American circus owner named P. T. Barnum (1810–1891) rented the fake mermaid. The body went on display in a museum, and a professor named Dr. Griffin explained the scientific link between these sea creatures and humans. The public paid to see the mermaid. Soon, the mermaid was once again exposed as a hoax. Dr. Griffin had been paid by Barnum to make up "facts" to convince the public that the mermaid was real.

P. T. Barnum became a very rich and famous man with his circus and exhibitions of "curiosities." He said that he saw nothing wrong in using "humbug," as long as the public was entertained and got value for money. By "humbug" he meant exaggeration and showmanship, but others might call his methods trickery. Barnum became widely known as the "Prince of Humbug."

MYSTERY HUNTER

Based on the evidence you have read in this chapter, do you think that mermaids and mermen exist? Using the information you have read, what scientific facts might support the theory that mermaids are real? Give reasons for your answer.

This portrait of P. T. Barnum shows him as a hum "bug"!

Chapter 4

EARTH AND BEYOND

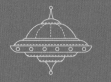

Scientists are always finding new evidence to support the idea that there is life on other planets, and to explain the beginnings of life on Earth. Everyone's fascination with the subject has given hoaxers perfect opportunities to trick scientists, historians, and the general public. For every ten real discoveries, there have been just as many hoaxes!

Alien Alert

Imagine driving along a rural road with your family one evening, when you suddenly spot a strange-looking figure. As you approach, you can see it more closely. It is a blue man!

This is what was reported to have happened in Michigan in 1958. Over the course of a few weeks, several motorists reported that they had seen an alien from another planet. There were different descriptions of the figure. According to some, he looked small; to others, he looked huge. They all agreed that the figure was blue and definitely not human.

Have aliens landed in the world's empty deserts?

Looking for the Little Blue Man

A police search failed to reveal the identity of the "Little Blue Man." But then, three young Americans came forward: Jerry Sprague, Don Weiss, and LeRoy Schultz. They revealed they were behind the hoax that had caused newspaper **headlines** across the United States. Sprague had dressed up in long underwear, gloves, a sheet with eyeholes, and a football helmet to which the friends had attached glowing lights. To finish off the effect, they had sprayed the costume with glow-in-the-dark blue paint! No wonder people thought they saw an alien shining in the darkness.

At the time of the Little Blue Man hoax there had been many reported sightings of alien life and alien spaceships or objects, known as Unidentified Flying Objects, or UFOs. These had given the men the idea for the hoax.

Flying Saucer Panic

In 2010, a newspaper called *Al-Ghad* caused panic in Jordan, in the Middle East. The front page of the newspaper claimed that UFOs in the form of flying saucers had landed in the Jordanian town of Jafr. The saucers, carrying giant aliens, had lit up the skies. When they read the report, terrified people in Jafr kept their children home from school. The town's mayor even called in the army to help cope with the invasion. Can you guess what day the story was printed on? That's right, April Fools' Day!

The Cardiff Giant

In 1869, workers were digging a well on "Stub" Newell's farm in Cardiff, New York. They unearthed a gigantic and extraordinary find—the body of a 10-foot-tall (3-m) man, made of stone! Word soon spread, and people flocked to see the fossilized giant. There were so many visitors that Stub charged people an entrance fee.

A Fossilized Giant

Many people believed the giant, soon known as the Cardiff Giant, was a stone statue. Others thought he was an ancient fossilized giant, like those mentioned in the Bible's Book of Genesis, which says, "There were giants in the earth in those days." While the debate went on, Stub Newell continued to make money from his many visitors. Then some businessmen paid Newell for the giant, and displayed it in a museum in Syracuse, New York. There, the **paleontologist** Othniel C. Marsh (1831–1899) declared it a fake. He pointed out the chisel marks on the giant, noting that they would have worn away if it had been buried for a long time.

The Cardiff Giant was an elaborate and well-planned hoax.

Proven a Fake

A New York storekeeper named George Hull finally confessed that the giant was fake! He had paid stonemasons to carve it and had arranged with his cousin Stub Newell to bury it. Hull, who did not believe in God, had thought of the hoax in order to trick a **clergyman** who said he believed that there once had been giants living on Earth.

Even though they knew the Cardiff Giant was a hoax, people still flocked to see it! Hull and Newell succeeded in making a lot of money from their trick. Some years later, Hull tried to repeat the hoax with another giant, this time with a tail. However, this trick failed from the outset!

MYSTERIOUS FACTS

This is how the Cardiff Giant was made:

- It was carved from gypsum, a soft limy rock.

- Stonecutters rubbed the stone model with sand, water, ink, and sulfuric acid to make it look old.

- When finished, the giant weighed nearly 3,000 pounds (1,360 kg).

Piltdown Man

In 1859, the English scientist Charles Darwin (1809–1882) published his ideas about how all animals had evolved, or developed, over billions of years from simple lifeforms that lived in the sea. He backed up his theory with evidence from fossils and living animals. Darwin also explained that humans had evolved from apes. At the time, however, there was no fossil evidence to prove that part of his theory.

Finding the Missing Link

What scientists needed was a fossil of an ancient human-like creature that shared features with both its ape **ancestors** and its human descendants. The search began for evidence of this "missing link." In 1912, an **archaeologist** named Charles Dawson (1864–1916) claimed he had found part of a human-like skull near the village of Piltdown in Sussex, England.

Dawson contacted the Natural History Museum in London, and he and an expert from the museum began further investigation. Their search unearthed more pieces of skull, including a jawbone and teeth. They carried out tests on the skull pieces, and concluded that it belonged to a human-like creature that lived over 500,000 years ago. Although some scientists were unsure about "Piltdown Man," others believed that the missing link had finally been found!

In 1953, tests on the skull showed that "Piltdown Man" was put together from the bones of an orangutan and a human, along with fossilized chimpanzee teeth. Even today, no one is certain who put together the hoax, although many people suspect Charles Dawson.

This is a replica (copy) of the so-called Piltdown Man skull.

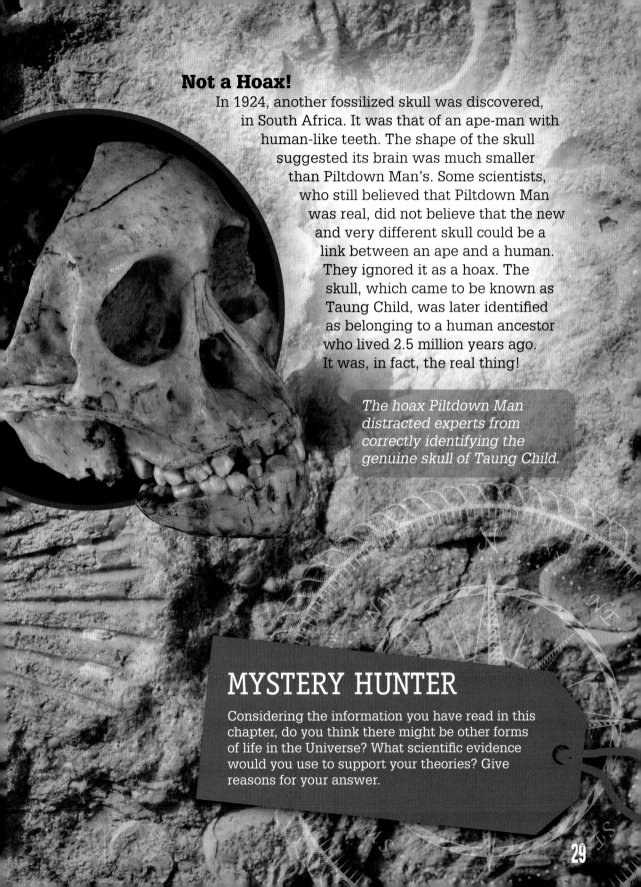

Not a Hoax!

In 1924, another fossilized skull was discovered, in South Africa. It was that of an ape-man with human-like teeth. The shape of the skull suggested its brain was much smaller than Piltdown Man's. Some scientists, who still believed that Piltdown Man was real, did not believe that the new and very different skull could be a link between an ape and a human. They ignored it as a hoax. The skull, which came to be known as Taung Child, was later identified as belonging to a human ancestor who lived 2.5 million years ago. It was, in fact, the real thing!

The hoax Piltdown Man distracted experts from correctly identifying the genuine skull of Taung Child.

MYSTERY HUNTER

Considering the information you have read in this chapter, do you think there might be other forms of life in the Universe? What scientific evidence would you use to support your theories? Give reasons for your answer.

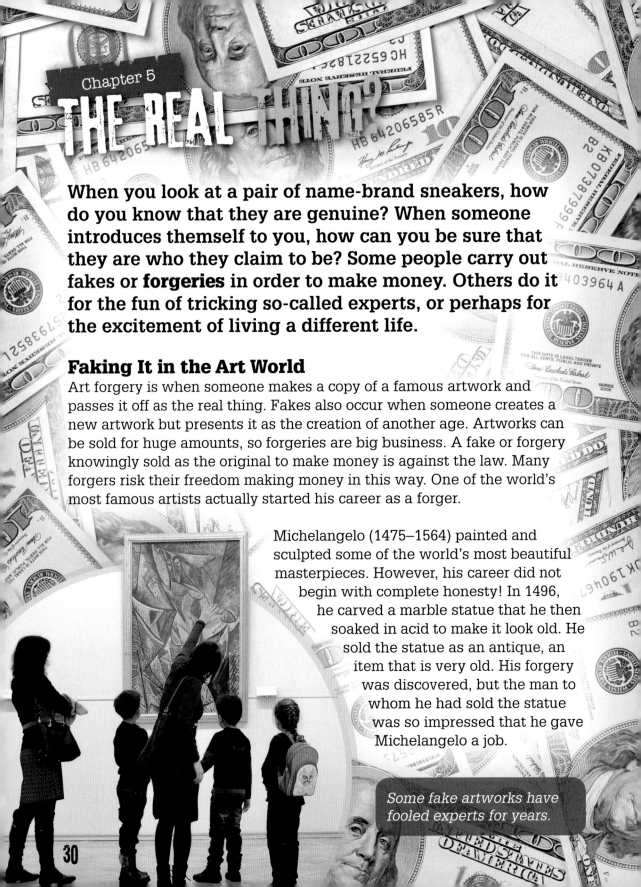

Chapter 5

THE REAL THING?

When you look at a pair of name-brand sneakers, how do you know that they are genuine? When someone introduces themself to you, how can you be sure that they are who they claim to be? Some people carry out fakes or **forgeries** in order to make money. Others do it for the fun of tricking so-called experts, or perhaps for the excitement of living a different life.

Faking It in the Art World

Art forgery is when someone makes a copy of a famous artwork and passes it off as the real thing. Fakes also occur when someone creates a new artwork but presents it as the creation of another age. Artworks can be sold for huge amounts, so forgeries are big business. A fake or forgery knowingly sold as the original to make money is against the law. Many forgers risk their freedom making money in this way. One of the world's most famous artists actually started his career as a forger.

Michelangelo (1475–1564) painted and sculpted some of the world's most beautiful masterpieces. However, his career did not begin with complete honesty! In 1496, he carved a marble statue that he then soaked in acid to make it look old. He sold the statue as an antique, an item that is very old. His forgery was discovered, but the man to whom he had sold the statue was so impressed that he gave Michelangelo a job.

Some fake artworks have fooled experts for years.

Imposter Alert

Some imposters trick people into believing they are someone else. Impersonating someone else to make money is a crime. One famous case of an imposter took place in 1817, when a confused young woman was found wandering through a village in Gloucestershire, England. She spoke a language no one could understand. Finally, a Portuguese sailor claimed to understand her. He explained she was a princess from the island of Javasu who had been kidnapped by pirates. She had leaped overboard and swum to shore. The story of "Princess Caraboo" was soon in all the newspapers. This was her undoing.

A woman came forward to say that she knew "Caraboo": the girl was, in fact, Mary Baker (1791–1864), the daughter of a shoemaker and born in Devon, England. The "princess" was actually a servant!

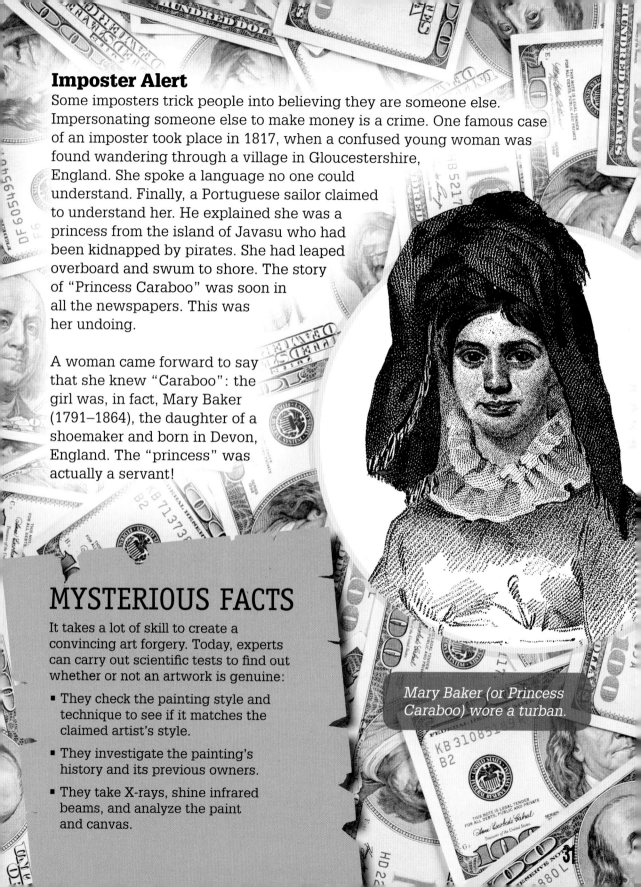

Mary Baker (or Princess Caraboo) wore a turban.

MYSTERIOUS FACTS

It takes a lot of skill to create a convincing art forgery. Today, experts can carry out scientific tests to find out whether or not an artwork is genuine:

- They check the painting style and technique to see if it matches the claimed artist's style.

- They investigate the painting's history and its previous owners.

- They take X-rays, shine infrared beams, and analyze the paint and canvas.

Faking It

Some works of art sell for millions of dollars. It is no surprise that artists sometimes work as forgers, copying artworks and trying to pass them off as the original. The earliest known forgeries were made by the ancient Romans, who copied older Greek artworks. Perhaps the most famous modern forger is Wolfgang Beltracchi (born 1951). He was sentenced to six years in jail in 2011 for forging 14 artworks, which sold for a total of $45 million.

A Load of Old Tea Bags

In 2014, Chinese painter Pei-Shen Qian (born 1940) was accused of forging works by famous modern artists such as Jackson Pollock, Mark Rothko, and Willem de Kooning. In order to make the alleged forgeries look real, he sometimes stained a new canvas with tea bags to make it seem older! Qian started his career in China, where he was paid to paint countless portraits of the then Chinese leader Chairman Mao, for display in public places. After arriving in the United States in 1981, he began a successful career as a forger. To avoid jail, he escaped back to China.

The stain from used tea bags makes things look old.

Copying the Copier

British painter and art restorer Tom Keating (1917–1984) admitted to creating thousands of copies of great artworks and selling them as originals. No one knows how many collectors of art possess Keating's imitations rather than the real thing. However, Keating's imitations now sell for a lot of money, even though buyers know they are forgeries of the originals. Other painters have even tried to copy Keating's copies and pass them off as his work!

Street Art

Banksy is a British graffiti artist who keeps his identity a secret. His art, sprayed onto walls, buildings, and bridges across the world, sells for hundreds of thousands of dollars. His work often comments on issues such as injustice, war, and poverty. Lots of street artists have copied Banksy's style. Sometimes people have great difficulty trying to figure out which is the real Banksy and which is a fake!

Is this the real Banksy or a fake?

Missing Princess

Anastasia Romanov was born in 1901 in Russia. She was the youngest daughter of the Russian ruler, Tsar Nicolas II, and his wife Aleksandra. Anastasia lived a comfortable life until 1917, when the Tsar lost power to **Communist** rebels. The Romanov family was taken captive. In July 1918, it was reported that they had all been shot dead in a basement. However, there were rumors that Anastasia had escaped the shooting.

Claims of a Princess

Since then, several women have claimed to be the princess. Among these was Anna Anderson. In 1920, Anna Anderson jumped off a bridge in Berlin, Germany, in an attempt to kill herself. She survived. She had no identification on her. She had bullet wounds and other scars on her body. She claimed she was Princess Anastasia.

The Romanov family is pictured here in 1914. Anastasia is sitting on the right, beside her father.

Anna said she had been carried out of the basement by two men, wounded but alive. According to her, she and her sisters had sewn jewels into their clothing to hide them from the Communists. She said she had been saved from death because the bullets fired at her hit the jewels. Many people disputed her claim, but Anna continued to say she was the princess. After her death in 1984, DNA tests revealed no connection between her and the Romanov family.

This photograph of Anastasia (right), her sister Tatiana, and dog Ortino was taken when they were in captivity.

The Sad Truth

In 1991, the site where the Romanov family was believed to be buried was dug up. Remains of the family's bodies were found, but Anastasia's could not be identified. Had the young woman really escaped? In 2007, archaeologists uncovered another burial site nearby. It contained the burned remains of at least two people. DNA tests concluded that the bodies were Anastasia and her brother, Alexei.

MYSTERIOUS FACTS

DNA is short for deoxyribonucleic acid. It carries all the information about how living things look and work:

- DNA is in every cell of every living thing.

- 99.9 percent of the DNA from two people will be identical. The remaining 0.1 percent varies from person to person. This is what makes us unique.

- The more closely related two people are, the more likely their DNA will be similar.

The Superhero

Sidd Finch was an incredible baseball star. Standing 6 feet 4 inches (1.93 m) tall, he took the New York Mets baseball team by storm. Yet he was torn between pursuing a career in baseball and his passion for yoga.

An Orphan

Finch, an orphan, began life in England. He was adopted by an archaeologist, who later died in a plane crash in Nepal. In his late teens, Finch went to the United States and studied briefly at Harvard University. Then he decided to become a **Buddhist** monk, so he dropped his studies to go to Tibet. There he spent time reflecting upon life by meditating. At the same time, he learned to pitch a baseball. However, Finch's pitch was out of the ordinary. His throws were incredibly fast—168 miles (270 km) per hour—and could hit far distant targets. News of Finch's skill traveled. Soon a manager for the Mets baseball team spotted Finch. He was amazed by the tall young man's ability.

Finch was quickly signed up to join the Mets. The player was unusual. He owned hardly any possessions apart from a musical instrument, a French horn, with which he was always photographed. For some reason, his trademark style was to have one foot bare and one wearing a work boot!

Sidd always carried his French horn.

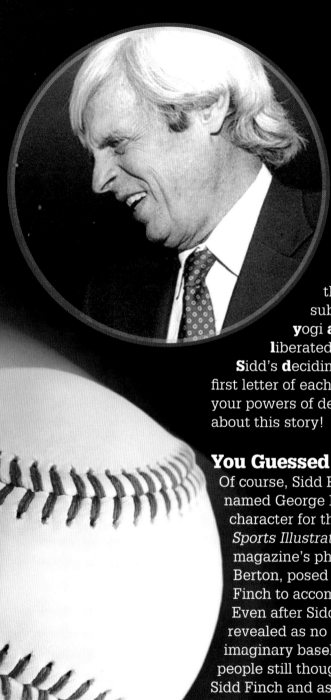

George Plimpton created the myth of superstar baseballer Finch.

The Truth

An article about Sidd Finch appeared in *Sports Illustrated* magazine in 1985. Underneath the article, there was a subheading: "**H**e's **a p**itcher, **p**art **y**ogi **a**nd **p**art **r**ecluse. **I**mpressively **l**iberated **f**rom **o**ur **o**pulent **l**ifestyle, **S**idd's **d**eciding **a**bout **y**oga ..." Look at the first letter of each word. What do they spell? Use your powers of detection to figure out the truth about this story!

You Guessed It!

Of course, Sidd Finch never existed! A journalist named George Plimpton created the character for the April 1 issue of *Sports Illustrated*. A friend of the magazine's photographer, Joe Berton, posed for photographs of Finch to accompany the article. Even after Sidd Finch was revealed as no more than an imaginary baseball superhero, people still thought Berton was Sidd Finch and asked for his autograph.

The Impostor

Today, Frank Abagnale advises others on **security** and how to protect themselves. But it was not always so! Born in 1948 in New York City, Frank began a career in fraud and forgery early in life. As a teenager, Abagnale put on a fancy-dress costume of a security guard. He stood by a security **deposit box** above which he had placed the sign: "Out of Service. Place deposits with security guard." Amazingly, people handed over their money!

Frank Abagnale advises people on spotting tricks and fakes.

Flying Around the World

When he was 16, Frank decided he would like to travel the world—without paying. He tricked an airline out of a pilot's uniform and employee **identity card**. He forged pilot qualifications and was soon flying around the world. Luckily, he was always the co-pilot and never controlled the plane. It is estimated that Abagnale flew on more than 250 flights to 25 countries!

Abagnale impersonated a pilot, but luckily he didn't take control of the plane.

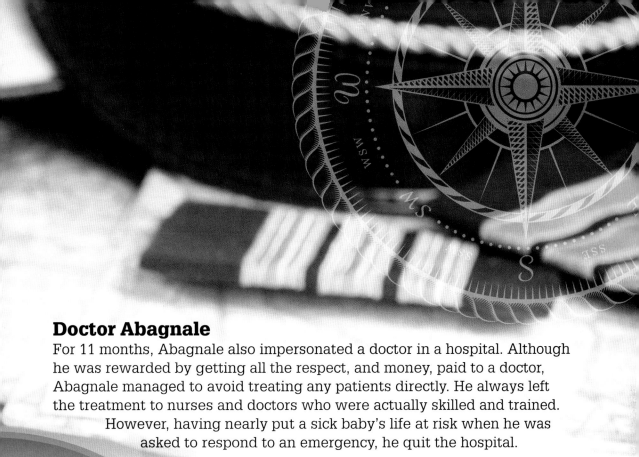

Doctor Abagnale

For 11 months, Abagnale also impersonated a doctor in a hospital. Although he was rewarded by getting all the respect, and money, paid to a doctor, Abagnale managed to avoid treating any patients directly. He always left the treatment to nurses and doctors who were actually skilled and trained. However, having nearly put a sick baby's life at risk when he was asked to respond to an emergency, he quit the hospital.

Abagnale was caught in 1969 when he was recognized by someone he knew from his time pretending to be a pilot. Abagnale served time in jail before being released on the condition that he would help the American police spot and stop similar frauds. In 2002, Leonardo di Caprio starred as Abagnale in a movie called *Catch Me If You Can*.

MYSTERY HUNTER

Using the information in this chapter, what clues would you look for to decide if something is a forgery, fake, or impersonation? Give reasons for your answer.

Chapter 6

MODERN FAKERY

People have been tricking each other for fun, to prove a point, or to make money for hundreds of years. Today, the Internet, social media, and computer **software** for altering photographs have opened up new opportunities for hoaxes and tricks. Some Internet fakes and forgeries are masterminded by criminal gangs to make money.

All for a Good Cause

Several well-respected newspapers reported in March 2015 that there was an amazing invention that turned water into wine. The idea was presented by two experienced businessmen. According to them, with their so-called Miracle Machine, a special **app** and water, anyone could make wine in their own kitchen. People **tweeted** about the machine in their thousands, and thousands more clicked on links on the businessmen's website to request more information about the product.

Days later, the newspapers admitted that they had been fooled. The whole thing was a publicity stunt for a charity. There was no Miracle Machine. The businessmen had played the prank in order to attract attention to their charity, Wine to Water. This raises money to provide clean water for the millions of people around the world who only have access to dirty, harmful water. The stunt was effective. Donations to the charity increased by 20 percent following the hoax.

Who would believe you could turn water into wine?

Do Not Be Conned!

There are many Internet hoaxes that are designed to get personal information from people. For example, people may receive an email claiming to be from their bank. If they click on a link to find out more, the victim will be asked to give their bank account number—which would be a very bad mistake indeed!

Criminals also make a profit by printing fake money. They use more and more sophisticated and complex ways to make money look real. Be careful that you are not conned! Simple checks can reveal if a dollar bill is genuine or not. The portrait should look clear—if details blend into the background, it is most likely a fake. Lines on the border of the bill should be clear and unbroken. Genuine currency paper has tiny red and blue fibers within the paper, but fake bills often have the red and blue printed on the surface. In stores and banks, ultraviolet light is often used to detect forged bank notes. Real bank notes have invisible markings that show up only in ultraviolet light.

Internet hoaxes can cause a lot of distress.

Faked Evidence

Today, it can be very hard to detect a fake image or hoax movie. Some people, such as those who are familiar with how special effects can be created using a computer, are automatically suspicious of everything they see. But, as has always been the case, others are more easily fooled.

Shark Attack

A photo of a shark seeming to jump up at a helicopter **went viral** on the Internet in 2001. It claimed to be *National Geographic*'s Photograph of the Year. Except it was not one photograph: it was two photos spliced together. The original photograph of the shark was taken by South African photographer Charles Maxwell. The photograph of the helicopter was taken by Lance Cheung. So far, no one knows who put together the fake photograph.

This is not the famous shark attack photo: it is one we put together! Were you fooled?

You would never believe penguins can fly. Or would you?

You'd Never Believe It But…

You probably know that penguins are birds that cannot fly. However, in 2005, filmmakers released incredible new footage of never-before-seen flying penguins. The short film showed a presenter in the icy Antarctic describing the flying creatures. Then the film showed the animals take off and head for the warmer climate of the rain forest. The hoax took a while to put together, before it was aired on … April 1, 2005!

To make the film, researchers found old but genuine footage of penguins in the Antarctic. Then, they set about looking at how they could seem to make them fly. They researched the way that similar animals fly and decided to base the penguins' flight on that of the guillemot bird. Using this information, they constructed a wire "flying penguin" model, which they used to create a computer-generated animation. The presenter was filmed in a studio with a wind machine and fake snow. Using special effects, the filmmakers put together all the elements so that it looked as if the penguins were flying.

Fake or Hoax?

People love to believe the unbelievable, and people love to prank. Always use your powers of detection to see if you can spot a hoax. Why do you think the hoaxer has chosen to carry out their plan—to make money, to gain attention, or just to make people laugh? And if you decide to carry out a hoax, make sure it is harmless and will not upset anyone.

MYSTERY HUNTER

Based on what you have read in this chapter, what evidence do you think can be used to figure out if a photograph or video is genuine? Do you think modern technology makes fakes and hoaxes harder or easier to carry out?

MYSTERY HUNTER ANSWERS

Chapter 1

Q *Based on the information you have read about the Angel of Mons, what historical evidence could you use to explain why the British public might want to believe in the visions? Give reasons for your answer.*

A World War I was a long and terrible war in which millions died on both sides. In 1914, British people would have been waiting nervously at home for news of their husbands and sons fighting in Europe. Perhaps the story of the angels gave them comfort.

Chapter 2

Q *Based on the evidence in this chapter, can you conclude that Bigfoot, the Yeti, and the Loch Ness monster are hoaxes, monsters, or unidentified species of animal?*

A There is as yet no definite proof that any of these options is the truth. The "monsters" have similarities to other animals. We also know that some people have reported fake sightings and manufactured fake "proof." However, without factual evidence, the question remains unanswered.

Chapter 3

Q *Based on the evidence you have read in this chapter, do you think that mermaids and mermen exist? Using the information you have read, what scientific facts might support the theory that mermaids are real? Give reasons for your answer.*

A There is as yet no reliable evidence that mermaids exist. There are no fossils of mermaids or other scientific proof of these creatures. However, modern discoveries of the coelacanth and other previously unknown species might suggest that there are still some creatures that are unknown to us.

Chapter 4

Q *Considering the information you have read in this chapter, do you think there might be other forms of life in the Universe? What scientific evidence would you use to support your theories? Give reasons for your answer.*

A Even though there have been countless hoaxes about alien life, that does not mean that it does not exist. The Universe is incomprehensibly large, and we are only just discovering the truth about our portion of it, the solar system. No life exists on any other planet in the solar system. However, considering all the many billions of planets in the Universe, perhaps we may one day discover that there is life out there.

Chapter 5

Q *Using the information in this chapter, what clues would you look for to decide if something is a forgery, fake, or impersonation? Give reasons for your answer.*

A Scientific evidence such as DNA testing can be used to check people's family connections. Other clues come from historical research. Stories such as that of Sidd Finch can be checked by researching the background for evidence of a person's existence. Thorough checks on Frank Abagnale's qualifications should have revealed them as forgeries.

Chapter 6

Q *Based on what you have read in this chapter, what evidence do you think can be used to figure out if a photograph or video is genuine? Do you think modern technology makes fakes and hoaxes harder or easier to carry out?*

A Evidence to discover fakes can come from scientific tests such as X-rays and chemical testing. Think about why a photographer would want to remain unknown for an incredible photograph. Search for further evidence from other experts—if there is only one source of evidence, it may be worth examining it more closely. Although computer trickery makes the creation of believable-seeming hoaxes easier to create, scientific testing and Internet searches can also make them easier to detect.

GLOSSARY

ancestors animals or humans from which others have descended

app software for a particular purpose

archaeologist someone who studies the past through examination of ruins, bones, and other remains

Buddhist follower of the religion based on the teachings of the Buddha

clergyman a priest

Communist political group that aims to establish an equal society without classes or money

cryptids animals whose existence has not been proven by scientific evidence

dark room room used by photographers to develop photographic film

deposit box place to securely put valuables

descendant someone who comes from a particular ancestor

evidence facts that can prove a belief to be true

fantasy of the imagination

footage part of a film recording

forgeries fakes or copies

fossils remains of living things that have been buried and gradually changed into a stony substance

headlines headings in a newspaper

hoaxes attempts to trick people

identity card card with personal details, used as proof of who a person is

legend traditional story that some people believe is based in fact

luger someone who takes part in the sport of luge

mammals particular class of animals, which includes humans, dogs, and lions

myths traditional stories

naturalist a scientist who studies animals and plants

paleontologist a scientist who studies fossils

pranks tricks

security ways to keep safe

social media websites and apps to share information and chat

software program or operating system used by a computer

sonar method of detecting objects underwater using sound waves

special effects in movies, making something look more believable or fantastic

species group of animals that look similar and behave similarly, and can breed together

supernatural forces that are beyond scientific understanding

tradition custom or way of doing something for a long time

tweeted posted a message on the social media website Twitter

went viral when something on the Internet becomes very popular and is shared many times

FOR MORE INFORMATION

BOOKS

Editors of Yes Mag. *Hoaxed!: Fakes and Mistakes in the World of Science.* Toronto, Canada: Kids Can Press, 2009.

Furgang, Kathy. *Fact or Fib?: A Challenging Game of True or False.* New York: Sterling Children's Books, 2014.

Levete, Sarah. *Science Fact or Fiction? You Decide!* New York: Crabtree, 2010.

Pasco, Elaine. *Fooled You!: Fakes and Hoaxes Through the Years.* New York: Square Fish, 2016.

WEBSITES

Find out about mythical and magical creatures:
www.factmonster.com/ipka/A0768922.html

For more about myths and legends, such as dragons and unicorns:
www.q-files.com/culture/myths-and-legends

Here's some more information about staying safe on the Internet:
www.safetynetkids.org.uk/personal-safety/staying-safe-online

Read more about Anastasia and the Romanovs:
www.biography.com/people/anastasia-9184008

Publisher's note to educators and parents: Our editors have carefully reviewed these websites to ensure that they are suitable for students. Many websites change frequently, however, and we cannot guarantee that a site's future contents will continue to meet our high standards of quality and educational value. Be advised that students should be closely supervised whenever they access the Internet.

INDEX